Lions Don't Eat Us

Lions Don't Eat Us

Constance Quarterman Bridges

 Winner of the 2005 Cave Canem Poetry Prize

Selected and Introduced by Sonia Sanchez

Graywolf Press
Saint Paul, Minnesota

Publication of this volume is made possible in part by a grant
provided by the Minnesota State Arts Board, through an
appropriation by the Minnesota State Legislature; a grant from
the Wells Fargo Foundation Minnesota; and a grant from
the National Endowment for the Arts, which believes that a
great nation deserves great art. Significant support has also
been provided by the Bush Foundation; Target; the McKnight
Foundation; and other generous contributions from foundations,
corporations, and individuals. To these organizations and
individuals we offer our heartfelt thanks.

Supported by the Jerome Foundation in celebration of the
Jerome Hill Centennial and in recognition of the valuable
cultural contributions of artists to society

Published by Graywolf Press
2402 University Avenue, Suite 203
Saint Paul, Minnesota 55114
All rights reserved.

www.graywolfpress.org

Published in the United States of America

ISBN-13: 978-1-55597-454-1
ISBN-10: 1-55597-454-6

2 4 6 8 9 7 5 3 1
First Graywolf Printing, 2006

Library of Congress Control Number: 2006924336

Cover design: Christa Schoenbrodt, Studio Haus

Cover photograph: "I obtained the kente at Bonwire in Ghana
in August 1996. The cloth was woven by the Ashanti. The Chief
selected it for me and said it signified beauty, health, and wealth."
—*Constance Quarterman Bridges*

Acknowledgments

I am grateful to the NEW JERSEY STATE
COUNCIL ON THE ARTS for a 1999 fellowship,
which enabled me to visit Dovedale in Charlottesville,
Virginia. The present owner, Colquitt Shackelford, Jr.,
grandson of the owner when my great-grandfather
worked there, graciously shared family ledgers of bar-
tering transactions between my great-grandfather and
his grandfather, Dr. Shackelford. This information
helped to confirm my mother's stories. In addition the
fellowship allowed me to visit family and the archives
in Richmond, Virginia, where I found more informa-
tion. My second fellowship award in 2005 will allow
me to visit the Low Country, my father's home.

Thanks to funds from my fellowship, recent DNA
testing showed that Daddy's people, the Quartermans,
descended from the Bini, Nigeria. These slaves were
left on the coast of Georgia and South Carolina and
became a part of the Gullah culture. Maternal DNA
testing shows that my great-grandmother Rhoda came
from the Songhai people of Mali.

Special thanks to The First Thursday Workshop, my
fellow writers, for their comments and support, and
to Peter Murphy, my guide into what is relevant to the
poem. Thank you, Laurie Kirk, my first poetry mentor
and J. C. Todd, my mentor when I entered the New

Jersey State Council on the Arts *Writers in the Schools Program*. J. C. continues to be mentor and friend with a keen editorial eye.

Thank you, loyal friend, Alice Bayne, for your friendship and editorial comments. Thank you, family supporters, especially, *sister-cousin* Kristin Lattany. Trina Byrd, my computer angel, thank you. To all ancestors, family, and future generations, this book is dedicated. Blessings on the Journey.

"Braiding" was published in *Black Diaspora*, Winter 2000. "Rhoda's Song" and "Gordian Knot" were published in the Fall 1999 issue of *Potomac Review*. "Gordian Knot" was selected to be published in *The Oxford Anthology of African American Poetry*. It was also one of the poems in the feature article on *The Oxford Anthology of African American Poetry* in *American Legacy*, October 2005. "Plowing" was published in the Summer 2002 issue of *African American Review*. "Her Way" won first prize in 2004's *Talented and Creative Ink* magazine. "Blood of Our Mothers" and "The Journey Home" were published in *Orison* XI, Winter 2005.

Contents

Part II

WEAVING AND THE WEAVERS

Part III
JOURNEYS

Part IV
ANCESTORS' STORIES, MYTHS, AND RITUALS

Introduction
by Sonia Sanchez

Someone said, there is a dance in each one of us. I would say there is also Moon. Prayer. Rain. Light and River. A river of castanets feeling the pulse of this book.

This is a book about hands, I think, enslaved men and women whose hands discovered life through shifting the earth. Hands wrapped in risks as they reached out for freedom:

Ellen, between her washing
and ironing on Dovedale,
spoke against slavery, had opinions
in a time when women were seen
and not heard. Her words scattered
discontent in the evening of a dying time.

This is a book about hands, I know, hands singing colors as they washed the feet of this country:

Old Man Fray always matched his mules
precisely like fitted pieces of a puzzle.
The horses at the mill were perfect pairs.
So it was not too far for him to travel
from his valley over blue mountains
to a distant Virginia county
where Randolph slaves were darker,

with molasses-colored Songhai skin,
African kinked hair and mahogany eyes.

He wanted to untie the weave
of the Gordian Knot. . . .

What to say to you now, pale skin Albert, as you
move across the scent of tongues:

I am his son. I am not his son.
I am slave; I am not slave.
I am man-child; I am child.
. . . .
My spirit is ragged with anger.
I am the coil of a serpent.

What song to sing to you now, African Rhoda, in
this still morning air, chained:

(. . .) like a storm you came.
Contained fury bound up
in a body you do not own.
. . . .
In a cave of Black Night, I will sing
to you a whip-poor-will's song.
I will hollow out a place where
freedom is reborn with each dawn
over these fertile Virginia farms.

This is a book about feet journeying, migrations
of a people, who walked a thousand midnights and
anointed their eyes with indigo:

Black families left the south with
burning in their bodies. It was not
a fever but fire paper-fed.

....

Fueled by words of *The Chicago Defender:*
lynching, low wages, southern funerals,
despair erupted into something tangible.

Nicolás Guillén wrote: "We have to learn to re-
member what the clouds cannot forget."

And these American clouds remind us that black
ribbons caressed the enslaver's hands as we observed
ourselves in an unfamiliar city. They thought we knew
nothing. Felt nothing. But we knew. But we knew high
above our heads the sky was blue, below the water
was singing death. We knew why the North Star pre-
ferred to shine brightest in the south. We knew how
our bodies were attuned to comets. We knew how our
tongues, arithmetic wonders, vibrated equations.

Behold the ancestor, remembering us of our
Native American flesh:

In a valley in Virginia
Great-Grandfather, red
with southern dirt,
wooed earth for crops.
His first cabin squatted
by fragrant fields
of tobacco leaves.
His Cherokee eyes
squinted to test sun strength
as he braided and bound
his long black hair.

Behold the ancestor, singing us myths:

From the land of things
which do not sleep
from the crown
of green mountain hair
of the Thunder god
comes Thunderbird.
Her shadow
is the storm cloud.
Wind screams her flight.

Behold the ancestor, summoning us to despoilers:
saying our blood would never keep us slave.
Behold the ancestor, translating the history:

Hidden by the lush pregnant
bulge of Cape Verde
is Île de Gorée
where slave houses,
called castles, cling like sores
on the body of Mother Africa.
Gorée, once called "Goede Reede,"
translated Safe Haven,
is child of barter and trade.

Miguel de Unamuno believed that by probing
deeply the character of men (women) belonging to a
time and a place, one can discover what is universal
and common to all men (women), what constitutes the
brotherhood of the race. . . .

Thank you my sister for your poems that help us
to see others and ourselves as we move to answer the
most important question of the twenty-first century:
What does it mean to be human?

Behold the ancestor and lions will never eat us.

Lions Don't Eat Us

Part I

 Blending

I am all of them, they are all of me

—Etheridge Knight, "The Idea of Ancestry"

ALBERT'S STORY
Part 1
Gordian Knot

Great-Grandfather Fray was a white man. He went to another Virginia county to get Grandpa Albert (his own mixed son) a wife. He wanted a dark-skin woman because Grandpa looked white.

—Aunt Edna

Old Man Fray always matched his mules
precisely like fitted pieces of a puzzle.
The horses at the mill were perfect pairs.
So it was not too far for him to travel
from his valley over blue mountains
to a distant Virginia county
where Randolph slaves were darker,

with molasses-colored Songhai skin,
African kinked hair and mahogany eyes.
He wanted to untie the weave
of the Gordian Knot, complicated
tangle he had created, with the issue
of silk-haired Albert, his son,
too fair to hide among the varied blacks.

The journey was apology or shame.
But cut or unwoven, the knotted
weave leaves kinks too deep

to hide or smooth away. Great-Grandma Rhoda, the woman Old Man Fray found, opulent with African genes, richly colored the complex threads of our generations.

ALBERT'S STORY
Part 2
The Me That Is

Therefore I will not refrain my mouth;
I will speak in the anguish of my spirit;
I will complain in the bitterness of my soul.

—Job 7:11

I am Albert out of Old Man Fray.
His white skin wraps the Africa
in me, which is honey.
African Mother, I am your egg.
Was I stolen from your nest?
My teeth have bitten bitter fruit.
Mother, your blackness dances
light into my veins.
I am an eaglet in a robin's nest.
My flesh is your flesh.
I am his son. I am not his son.
I am slave; I am not slave.
I am man-child; I am child.
I clatter in loud silences of me.
In early morning and night scents
I smell freedom.
I see free birds soar even
in gray skies.
I see how foxes return
to their own holes.
My cries return unanswered,

cotton seeds on untilled fields.
Grief is my bedfellow.
It grabs me, tosses me in the night.
My spirit is ragged with anger.
I am the coil of a serpent.

ALBERT'S STORY
Part 3
Old Man Fray

My father, Old Man Fray,
has come home
like a warrior from battle.
He brings you, a trophy, for me.
Girl, my ears tasted your cries
among wheel-scrape noises
on our roadway stone.
Your cries from his wagon a warning,
chains dragged on silence.
Does he know what he's brought home?

Not a broad wife,*
but a broad-winged hawk trapped
by wisps of pinfeathers.
Girl, you know the taste of sky.
Loosed, you'll fly away even though
we know the price.
Still he puts your tether in my hands.
Can I hold the tugs of your flight?
Does he know what he has brought?
Black field-ripened blackberry;

Rhoda, he calls you. How can he name
a hawk, with wings, flight, and distance

* *broad wife: female slave whose husband was owned
by another master*

mirrored in your keen eyes?
He must not know talons
which can grab and scratch out
breath-wind of life. Rhoda,
how will you see my unbaked skin?
Your eyes know shapes
and texture of hunting.
Your hawk-eyes know prey.

ALBERT'S STORY
Part 4
The Courtship

Rhoda, my She-Hawk,
like a storm you came.
Contained fury bound up
in a body you do not own.
Your eyes are hurricanes,
they flatten my world.
Still I want to taste your scent.
Rhoda, come lie with me.

Rhoda, I am familiar, like earth.
I will feed you from concealed
waters where I keep dreams,
passed by drums vibrating
from sweet black fingers
of my mother and grandmothers.

Come, teach my body flight
beyond these Virginia fields.
We will survive.
Show me to hunt on wing.
Teach my tongue to say your name
Rhoda, She-Hawk.
I promise eternal love to you.

Shush. Don't cry.
In a cave of black night, I will sing
to you a whip-poor-will's song.

I will hollow out a place where
freedom is reborn with each dawn
over these fertile Virginia farms.
Come, my love, jump over the
broom with me.

Chocolate

Great-Grandfather Albert, in later years
called his wife, my great-grandmother Rhoda,
Chocolate; tall molasses-smelling woman,
from the plantation of the Randolphs'.

Light chocolate liquid eyes, dark
chocolate body, long-legged, erect farm girl,
tallest among women on that Virginia farm;
her hair flashed blue-black sparks, defiant

fire from her African roots. Reluctant,
feet planted, selected and taken for Albert's
bride, her hands became claws and protested
that trip to the house of a stranger.

Easter is the time of their marriage, pale Albert
and chocolate Rhoda full of colored eggs
sons, daughters, my grandfather Austin.
Rhoda resurrected by marriage. Resurrected!

RHODA RANDOLPH FRAY
Part 1
Rhoda's Song

(Great-Grandma Rhoda died Nov. 8, 1911.)
Grandma took in laundry for white folks . . .
I remember she had a fluting machine and did
fancy ironing like ruffles and fluting to help
Grandpa acquire land for their five children . . .
I also remember there was some talk of another
child before she came to Grandpa. I don't know.
I was little.

—Mother

It never left her, the scent
and marks of yellow lye soap
she used to scrub clean
laundry for the white ladies
in plantations on the hill.
The lie, on her hands, stayed.
It still clung to her, the sweet

baby scent of her firstborn son
sent away with the runaway
slave girl, Sara, on the night
he was born, blood-washed,
baptized with Rhoda's pain.
The moon hid from her lesser shame.
Dark blanketed the northern route.

It never left her, the sorrowful
tune she sang in filtered sunlight
by the empty grave of the son
Rhoda named Dahomey,
that name whispered to her
by night voices in half dreams.
It never left her, the shape

of the small white cross,
as white as ruffles and flutes
crimped into stiff shapes
with her fluting machine.
The cross has peeled, gone back
to ashes, leached ashes, to make
lye soap for washing away.

RHODA RANDOLPH FRAY
Part 2
Patience

She was the greatest grandma on earth, so
sweet, had lots of patience with us. She was
always on our side . . . It seemed the more
noise we made, the happier she was rocking
in her chair.

—Mother

Time trembled on Rhoda's tongue.
She thought maybe stillness
would make invisible the woman's
body she did not own.

She became a drawn, quiet breath
captured in the well of her heart.
Still the man came to take her away.
No one cared what she would leave

or who the boy was lingering
by the lip of road with winter's ice
in his eyes or how his huge hands
squeezed air behind his back.

Her pleas were ignored like gnats
dotting the air and her cries
were but the noise insects make
in their futile minuets.

Transported, this young girl,
still musky like plowed fields,
thought this new boy is too fair,
too far away from the familiar.

Later, in quiet, patient times,
in her rocker she dreamed
her way back where patience was born.
In bound straws of the broom

Rhoda jumped over to be Albert's bride,
she was the unbound reed stuck out
not strong enough to trip over, but sharp
enough to nick, scratch, and leave a mark.

RHODA RANDOLPH FRAY
Part 3
This Is My Silence

I say this in my head
even if I could hide in a city
of tongues
I would not speak this.
Old Man Fray brought me here
from between red thighs
of Virginia mountains
for his son, Albert, with pale skin,
gray, early-morning eyes.
Black blood boils in Albert.
A coal fire smolders underground.
I have my own old sorrows.
But years have softened my heart
like worked dough on a breadboard
and that strange boy, Albert,
has risen up a man, has loved me,
fathered our children, Austin,
Rosa, John, Alice, and Mary
from the same womb
used by that first lost child, now
with grown-up arms and legs.

How can I find him, a feather
carried away on north winds?
How can I follow the flight
of moving birds?
Sometimes in a pause at the edge
of my energy, I look up to blue sky
and wonder if I don't get too drunk
with blue and space, and had wings
would my wingspan
be wide enough to carry all I love?
If I had wings, would my wingspan
mount the air to carry me far enough
to find what I have lost?

Damaged by Wind

At Beulah Baptist Church
in Friday Prayer Meeting
women in their corsets
and summer bonnets
fidget in pews. Pass whispers
between opening hymns
and prayers. Whispering
and murmers slither over
Rhoda, find her,
rest on her shoulders.

That night in their bed
Rhoda carefully places phrases
on her husband's pillow among
soft feathers. Albert's words
are reassuring, innocent.
She chews his words. Unsatisfied
she reaches for comfort of sleep
but it will not come to her.
This muggy pre-storm night
Rhoda is tormented by doubts

as persistent as the wind that
assaults their home, scratching
and pulling at eaves.
Finally dawn and the cock's crow
intrudes with a façade of tranquility.

At breakfast, bacon chokes her.
She watches Albert in his fields
hip-deep in what he has planted.
Morning grits and eggs are pebbles
in her stomach.

Cranky red hens dry their wings
in the sun, cackle, follow roosters.
Everywhere there is happy coupling.
Bees make love to poppies, to bees.
Yellow black-eyed Susans
watch Rhoda in her Sunday-
Going-to-Meeting bonnet punish
the front gate. Her feet tramp
red dirt puffs on the road to town.
That evening on her way back home

crickets serenade in harmony.
Rhoda hums, steps over storm debris.
At her neighbors' kitchen windows
starched curtains are moved slightly
like shifting of dry cattails in wind
before a storm. Watching bangs
against windowpanes.
There is waiting in the air.
Rhoda, erect in her indignation
holds corset-tight words of discovery.

She places sentences in her palms,
squeezes, puts them in her pockets.
Fists.
At home in the cool of their porch
Albert waits, waves,
offers a tentative smile.
Rhoda's words punch
and fracture the evening air.
Albert, I saw your bastard son.

Rhoda's Face

Show me your face, Rhoda.
Did you think I would not find you
in pictures you refused to take?
In splinters of night your face appears
to me, sweet African woman, stifled-
song woman with unheard poetry.
Great-Grandmother, I know you.
I know your scent, lilacs,
Mother said you loved them.
I know your face we keep it in family
on our children's faces.
I know your voice, lullaby soft,
my mother sang your songs.
Proud, tall, Songhai woman
you could barely read
but you became a reservoir for words
in your hoarded books.
Your grandchildren read from books
softened by your caresses.
I know words you did not speak
they struggled to be born.
Poetry lived behind your closed lips
and danced behind your eyes.
Your words were not stillborn
they just waited to be later
on the tongues of our children.

Cheawanta's Dance

Ellen and James Lewis meet.

Sisi-wan, sisi-wan, it is the way
of wind in oaks feathering leaves.

Cheawanta* weaves her nest in the eaves.
Her body is full of bright blue promises.

She pauses, rests on the girl's veranda.
In a mulberry nearby, cheawanta puffed

feathers darker than the berries, waits,
practices his mating dance.

The young man gathers accoondews,
hazy blue berries, to juice the tongue.

Under the Virginia sky warm kisses
of sun and breeze trace his body.

He raises his new boot, smiles, and taps
tobacco from his still warm pipe.

He slips it gently into his shirt pocket.
It rests against his racing heart

as he strides toward the yellow house
of the girl with the magnetic, dark eyes.

* Cheawanta: Powhatan Indian word for robin

The gathered morning eggs, culled,
wait for market on her porch.

Hulled spring peas, cupped in her apron
roll. The girl stills her mother's rocker

rises to begin the journey
of my blood.

Remembering James Lewis

(James Lewis died March 31, 1917.)
April 2000 we visited Dovedale, where we saw
the barter records. We then visited the family
home place in Stony Point, Virginia.

I could sing Great-Grandfather James Lewis
like a folksong. I could say how women
loved him as they loved First Sunday,
Virginia ham, and new bonnets.
I could say his hands were light
as they gathered reed to weave
chair bottoms and baskets.
Or I could say how the earth yielded to him
as the women did before he married Ellen.
I could say he was a Bishop blessing his land
before he broke it into pieces, sacrament,
for his children, *still our land, sweat-soaked,*
blood-fertilized, holy with babies' bones.
But I believe he would say, know me
this way from the Shackelford Barter Records:
June 22, 1867—one half mutton for winter
June 19, 1868—money lent to pay
    for Sanford's shoes
May 21 and 25, 1871—Doctor's visits
    for the children

June 10, 1871—one and one half day's work
    one dollar
August 21, 1871—planks for a coffin
    by George Tyree for the baby
March 27, 1872—prescriptions for son James
February 26, 1875—hired horse, (named) Bob,
    and steers to move house
July 12, 1882—lent horses to haul wheat
August 5, 1883—doctor's visit for baby Charles.
July 2, 1885—doctor at birth of Eliza's child
January 3, 1899—pay for day's work by Charles
> *Know, that I am just a man,*
> *James Lewis, tired, an old workhorse.*
> *I am red clay, overfarmed land*
> *forgettable as the color of rain. Will you*
> *remember the land, on which you stand,*
> *my daughter Elenor's, your grandparents'*
> *and remember that which pulls you home?*

James Lewis's Hands

My Grand (James Lewis) loved her (Ellen)
very much even though he had many lady
friends.

—Mother's Journal

James loved the ladies.
The women came with pies, oozed
words, as sticky as their pies.
They brought fresh churned butter,
thick and fluffy as summer clouds.
They buzzed and rubbed their legs
together, queen bees, drunk with want,
drawn to honey of his Cherokee tongue
and deep-set, promising, midnight eyes.
Even after James went to Staunton, Virginia,
miles away, brought Ellen to his marriage
bed, women came, as surely as seasons.
They followed James to his ripe fields,
shadows trailing a summer sun.
There he hummed, but never sang.

His long lean shadow cast him larger
as he stroked tobacco leaves with strong
brown hands; his eyes stroked them.
They watched his hands weave baskets,
pull cane for chair bottoms, tried to will

his hands on them even for a moment.
Evenings his fingers wandered the curve
of Ellen's neck and throat.
They entangled themselves in her hair,
made love to her lips and eyes, followed
familiar paths of her varied textures.
His warm lips and body in full and varied
tones sang his love songs for her.
Night ears heard him say, *Beloved El.*
She whispered her name for him, *Song Bird.*

Sunday Silk

Ellen was a quiet woman very dignified, put
every word in its place, was fashionable, polite
to everyone . . . I thought too much (niceness)
to some

—Mother's Journal

Ellen was black cotton hair, a look
of moccasin trails and Sunday silk.
She smiled love on James,
was his morning song, filled his nose
and eyes like sun-ripened fruit.
Women "sat tea" with Ellen, studied her,
looked for what she had that enticed
the eyes of James.
They wondered if Ellen could be erased
like a mistake in figuring numbers
or blotted out like an annoying smudge
on clean paper of *figuring,*
wondered if with persistent presence
they could break her, like one breaks a colt.
While visiting, a woman I'll call Annabella
put poison in Ellen's tea.
The doctor saved Ellen's life, told James,
Be careful. James loaded his shotgun, rode
Old Nellie, his horse, became death on wind,
became judgment day. He called Annabella

to come out from her house. In the silence
he told her if she came back
to their home, he would shoot her on sight
like possums he hunted in fields.
His hand trembled on the hair trigger.
Annabella's parlor lamp went out.
James went home for his love of Ellen.

A Proper Woman

*Grandma Ellen was put off Dovedale for
speaking against slavery. That's when she and
Grandpa, James Lewis, acquired their land. I
guess you can say they were thrown out of slavery.*

—Aunt Edna

Ellen wore her quietness
like a Sunday bonnet,
with satin ribbons loosely tied
beneath her chin. She was dignity,
a free, proper woman, in improper
times. Ellen was grit in eyes
of a south, dredged in slavery
and inhabited by quiet women both
Black and white who wore shells
of gentility that covered toughness.
Their practiced honey-smiles were glue
of southern decorum and graciousness.
Ellen, between her washing
and ironing on Dovedale,
spoke against slavery, had opinions
in a time when women were seen
and not heard. Her words scattered
discontent in the evening of a dying time.
Some say Ellen's words caused change,
pitchforks pushed into layers of earth.

This Day

Ellen Lewis died Oct. 31, 1912.

At the tip end of October
this day is fertile, pulsates
like a heartbeat, is full
pregnant-woman round
tight with ripened life.

Pumpkins lie in dying fields
like plump orange dots
on a brown plush dress.
Corn is in yellow piles
heaped hills in a full barn

of meat, promises and husks.
But in the memory of trees,
in the constant, winter waits.
On the back steps of Ellen's
house, loud spicy essence

of burned tobacco fields
meets quieter pungent scents
of cinnamon and mace
which have escaped from
her scalding pots.

On her kitchen table
a last gathering of apples,

fragrant red and yellow
spheres, spill on the white
oilcloth.

The black cookstove pops,
chatters, with a belly full
of fat chunks of firewood,
glows red like a setting sun.
Drops of escaped water

from steaming pots sizzle
on the stovetop
while canning jars dance
in the music of steam.
Her husband, James,

is in the field sawing firewood
for the bin by the kitchen door.
He pauses, smiles at the day.
In her kitchen Ellen wipes
perspiration from her face.

She wonders at the sudden
tightness in her breast,
as she slides gently from her chair
a fluttering leaf of autumn.
James does not hear the clatter

of chair on the oak floor
nor her final sigh as delicate
as the work of bird wings
on the countenance of a breeze.
When James returns, he touches

her face, remembers how winter is.
On his horse he is silent, rides
to the doctor's house, rides
away from her, away from that
which he cannot plow, cut, or split.

His horse's shoes fly off, missiles,
upward toward a God
James has never understood.
This day with clenched fists
which hold the reins, he wants
to smash the face of God.

Part II

 ### Weaving and the Weavers

WEAVE: to interlace and form by combining various elements to make a whole

What makes us African Americans is the blending of blood. We are and will always be most strongly African. We are a beautiful and diverse people because of this blending.

> *While Europeans forcefully entered the African blood stream, Native Americans and Africans merged by choice, invitation and love. This profound difference cannot be understated and it explains why families who share this bi-racial inheritance feel so much solace and pride.*
>
> —William Loren Katz,
> *Black Indians: A Hidden Heritage*

The Food of Storytelling

In the warmth of the cookstove
Mother was the *truth keeper* who sat
cross-legged on the kitchen floor,
a tidy woman among untidy children
telling family stories. It was a gift her
grandparents gave her by dying campfires.

Talking about family was delicious to her.
Forgotten was her day of doing laundry
on scrub boards in tin tubs, clothes drying
into frozen shapes on clotheslines and flat
irons heated spit-hot on a coal stove.
Lines disappeared from her face.

Sometimes at the end of the day a wisp
of hair escaped from severe hairpins.
Hair forgotten and her soiled apron folded
she held us with her voice and passion.
Her transformed face told us she was back
in the arms of Virginia, her home.

Mother's stories thick with body were like
Karo syrup she put on Sunday pancakes.
Sometimes when I am alone I think
about the nature of food, how it comforts,
nourishes eyes, spine, and bones.
I think of seeds and life in tiny fragments.

I think about what is needed for planting
and how unexpected summer storms
often come at night in dark deluge or mist,
how rain penetrates the pores of earth
and where water falls, even sparsely,
earth remembers and a new crop
grows with the remembering.

Where Wolves Live

Amanda, Cherokee, mother
to my grandmother, Fannie,
I am your great-granddaughter.
On the red trail from Georgia
I cry the trail from our ancestral home.
I see as massive as clouds, the white
wolves from tundra in the north.
I see family prodded like cattle
into the mouths of wolves.
I have been where the wolves live.
They carried your heart and liver
to their den and devoured them.
Among bleached brittle bones
I search for the shape of my face.

The Weavers' Threads

The ancestors are here.
They whisper in my ears, remind me:
The warp of me is the width of me
Cherokee wide.
The weft of me is the length of me
African long.
One Mother Spirit binds all earth
children born
of her soil, indigenous Americans
and Africans.
I sing of Cherokees. I sing
of Africans.
To ancestors I offer libation.
My poured
offering will honor them.
I have the African body of a Hottentot
woman, yellow-brown skin,
untamed hair, flat face, and tilted eyes.
I offer libation
to the ancestors.
The warp
of me is the interlaced
woven spirit of me.
My great-grandfather's Irish
moles
and Irish freckles

are not African but mine.
My buttocks,
full like the continent
of Africa, marks me African.
I'm presented not fully made
still on the weavers' loom
being pulled
and stretched by rhythmic male feet
of Kente weavers
by fingers
of weeping Cherokee women.

Photograph Album

Grandmother kept her album
on a pedestal beside her Bible.
I was three and knew they lived
on licorice-colored pages, faces
she called family; people
folded away like paper dolls,
her mamma, poppa, and sisters
prim in their Sunday best.
A young grandmother was there
on show-horses decorated
with first-place blue ribbons, in love
with Austin, my grandfather.
Charlie, her youngest brother,
tumbled sunshine from beneath
an upturned straw hat.
Pale-skin Albert was there without
African Rhoda. Later I can picture
Rhoda's face, the face she didn't
want recorded, recorded in Mother's
camera eyes. James and Ellen,
my great-grandparents,
are distinguished, in single photos.
These relatives Grandmother touched
with love and I mimicked her.
During summer visits when
Grandmother went gathering

in cool of summer afternoons
among corn, beans, and grapes
and as the chickens filled
with corn-cackled contentment
I would tip into her parlor
among mohair chairs, oriental rugs,
and heavy drapes, to visit family
who waited for me
in the grape-leaf green album.
Its raised velvet felt like undersides
of leaves in Grandmother's
wine grape arbor.
Family names became church
like Sunday School recitations
as in Genesis and Numbers.

Passing

On a summer-flushed day, cloudless-blue
and suffocated with sun, death came
to Aunt Vinnie in 1910 in Virginia.
They laid her out in the main parlor
among mohair furniture, under windows
with pulled-back blue velvet drapes.
The scent of lilacs and lemons dusted
camphor smells of the parlor.
In days following, people came
from miles around, remembered how

Vinnie's strawberry jam, her souse,
and smoked ham made love to tongues.
Persian rugs softened their footsteps.
Gloved hands to the mouth muffled words
about her dead white husband, about
gray-eyed daughters with golden hair.
Later on the porch in black crepe dresses
women perched like crows, gossiped about
Vinnie's porcelain skin, teacher-daughters
now tending the kitchen, lemonade and chicken.

After coffee and sweet potato pie they spoke
of darker daughters who remained home
and Lovie, the baby girl, who took a piece
of her mother's heart when she walked
the Charlottesville Road north with train fare

clutched in her pale hands for passage
to the capital, Washington, D.C.
Everyone saw Aunt Vinnie's sorrow, saw
her pain like a missing eye or finger.
No one spoke of this to her face

or about passing into another world
of privilege, acceptance, and assimilation.
On the last official day of mourning,
in anonymous dark night a black Ford
passed on the road near Aunt Vinnie's
house, a one-car funeral procession.
Strangers in the car, white faces. Dogs
did not bark either warning or greeting.
The next morning, an empty chair, out of place
at the head of Aunt Vinnie's ebony coffin.

Composition for Charlie

I remember Uncle Charlie. He was really
a Ladies' Man . . . true son of Grandpa,
James (Lewis)

—Aunt Edna

Charlie wore a tilted straw hat
and tilted smile.
It was said, love and wisdom
lived in the lank of him
like twin hearts.
I only know Great-Uncle Charlie
from my aunt's and mother's words
and his photograph, which
demands response like sudden
light on a dreary February day.
In his copper-tinted face, gray
eyes flash secrets and promises.

The men in town called him
Cockarouse Charlie, important
man, wise Virginia man
with knowledge of Cherokee ways:
how to twist a plug, how to work
magic with the power of words.
The women in the county said,
Charlie is an orchestra.

His sweet lips and tongue
are seductions of a saxophone.
He fingers all our strings:
violin, mandolin, bass, harp.

He fiddles a woman, makes her sing.
His body carries the beat
of native drums in smoky camps.
Between his birth, July 6, 1883
and his death, May 22, 1933
are captured only a few notes
of him—not intermezzo, but notes
which drift from behind windows
where a full orchestra is in recital.
Recorded in pencil on the Family
Scroll, tentative like a flute song
Charlie Lewis married last time, June 24, 1916.

Charlie's Women

You play us, Charlie.
You love our shapes
full-busted, big-hipped,
taut, ripe brown skins,
long slender necks,
Charlie's women.
We're your violins,
mandolins, and guitars.
You pluck our strings,
glide your bow
until music comes,
blue notes, jazz notes.
We hum, sing songs
you don't know.
We holler, Holy, holy!
You are so loved, Charlie,
but you are never
the music,
only the musician.

Two Days after the Fourth of July 2000

Charlie Lewis, son of Great-Grandfather James
(July 6, 1883–May 22, 1933)

Great-Uncle Charlie is in my yard
under the giant cedar tree
robins all around his feet, thirty
maybe forty.
I have never seen so many at once.
Great-Uncle Charlie walked
from his portrait one hundred eighteen
years after his birth.
In filtered sunlight he is telling his story.
He tips his wide straw hat, places
it to the back of his head.
Gray eyes sparkle in his sun-brushed skin.
Six feet of slenderness look down
at me, grin, say he was maligned.
He heard I was writing about him.
Says he was a writer, too, wrote poetry,
did not smoke, loved good liquor,
loved many ladies, they loved him back,
married three of them.
He walks down the driveway to the street
carrying the light with him in his smile.
His whistle startles the air.
I am suddenly empty as he strolls
from my sight back into his father's sperm.

Her Name Was Mary Fray

As a child, I remember three horses in our
family, Mary Smith, Mary Fray, and Frank.

—Aunt Edna

The night is cruel, rain bites
my hide like angry wasps,
flattens my mane, pushes
wet hair into my eyes,
but I'll carry you home, John.
Feet up. Feet down. Forward.
Feet up. Feet down. Forward.
Don't awaken, John!

They have sent us home again
from the warm bar and people
with you thrown over my back
like a brown sack of oats.
I know the way to our place.
Steady, feet. Steady!
My back leg hurts, bites
from that mean old dog, Jeff.

God bless this old Mary Fray.
God bless and watch over
all of us who walk on fours,
Mary Smith and Frank.
Trot pass Tucker's Woods,

but remember Skunk is there.
John, maybe I'll not take you home.
Maybe I'll go where they put

white crosses on the hill on Lewis
Farm. We planted your wife and babies
there after the fever finished them.
Feet up . . . Feet down . . .
I could take you to that place, John.
Remember I pulled the wagon,
which carried them in white boxes,
in smells of clover and time of flies.

Feet up . . . Feet down . . .
Watch out! Tom's Meadows.
Cottonmouth waits there! Sometimes,
I'm the only one caring for you, John.
Soon will be, Bog's Bridge.
It is old, worn, sways like a loose saddle.
It sighs and creaks like our barn.
Beneath is creek water my father loved.

But it swallowed him, like drink,
when he slipped off the bridge.
In the woods, I smell Deer.
She watches me.
John, I smell you. You stink.

You smell of bourbon, sweat, and me.
We are joined like six limbs to one body,
this old Cayuse and you.

Will you always love me, John?
When my legs and back are weak,
and bend and sway like wet straws
in the wind? Will you love me, John?
I'm your only compass.
I am the trusted safety you know.
John, should I nudge open your cottage door,
ease you down like a bundle of hay?

Or I could carry you to the valley
where my grandfather is buried, a forgotten
bone, left when he fell with your half naked,
howling grandfather. It was the day pale men
gobbled up our people's land, like feed.
John, we're at Bog's Bridge now.
Sleep, John. Sleep a little longer, John.
I could let you slip under the green
pond, like dawn slips under the shadows
of these Virginia hills.
One foot up . . .

Capacity to Love

My mother often said she wondered
if madness ran in our family
like an underground river.
She said this when I said
I wanted to be a poet
not a secretary. I wanted
words to be mine, not dictated.
Mother said her mother had a sister
who married a man she craved
like the taste
of her mamma's vanilla icing
on lemon chiffon cake.
Aunt Bea and he were committed,
showed it, held hands, touched
on public streets in the 1800s,
scandalized family and friends.
Her husband, Tom, died *with*
plague before his thirtieth birthday,
before the blessings of children.
Aunt Bea would not let go of his hand,
held Tom to her breast even in death,
as though she could breathe life
back into his failed lungs.
On a slate-colored April morning
Tom was buried in the family cemetery.

That night Aunt Bea stretched out
on soft damp earth; her body
like a blanket covered his grave.
The dew tears of night fell,
crumpled her funeral dress.
Morning came. She, as limp
as her crinolines, was carried away
to the sanatorium.
It is still whispered that her spirit
stayed with Tom and joined the wisps
one sees in Virginia in our family graveyard.
I never told my mother I want that madness.
I want that capacity to lie down
in pliant earth, my fear
of giving up self to a man for love,
to hold onto his hand
in death even until my own.

Grandmother Said

*Summers I stayed in the country with
my grandmother Elenor.*

I grew up with Grandmother's
Rhode Island reds
with brown eggs and arbor
grapes for white and red wines.

Life was seasoned with her
spices and Virginia ham.
I was made more aware
of feet, legs, mouth, and hands.

Idle hands are the devil's work.
Angels will watch over you.
Children should be seen not heard.
Speak up, why are you so shy?

Girl, don't track mud into my house
on your dirty shoes.
Keep your shoes on. Ladies
don't go barefoot.

Boogieman is out there, under
your window, in the holly bush,
gonna get you. Why are you crying?
Big girls don't cry.

There's nothing to be afraid of.
Don't ever let boys kiss you.
Be nice. One day you'll get married.
Keep your legs closed. Dance.

Her Way

I learned her ways in the summers
I vacationed with my grand-mom Elenor,
away from my parents' growing family.
Grand-Mom said seven children in the hands
of chance and in the city were too many
in murky times of the Depression.
Too busy growing food I liked:
butter beans, white corn, snap beans,
my grand-mom never said I love you.
On my three braids I wore her ironed ribbons
tied with love like gift finishing on a package.
Evenings she brushed tea into my unruly hair,
and grew me with country air and good food.
A child, it took me years to interpret her eyes,
her hands, the language of her fried chicken,
shoes without holes, and dresses sewn with love
by hands that never seemed to rest.
It has taken me most of my life to understand
the many faces love can wear.

The Walls Have Ears

There is a secret code: lifted brows,
narrowed eyes, pursed black lips,
cleared throat, feet scraped on the floor.
Walls have ears.

My parents knew *silent talk* from their parents.
With hooded eyes, steel–
chain grip on our arms we were taught
from infancy what was meant

by gestures, inclined heads, and blinked eyes.
We were told to speak softly about plans
and family business, which *stayed in the house.*
I remember my summers in rural Washington, D. C.

My grandmother pulled window shades
when Grandfather came home from work;
they communicated with nods, looks,
and gestures as she discussed her day.

My grandmother's mother in Virginia learned
this language from the old people chained
by plantation codes of secrecy. African drums
were silenced but not eyes.

The cabin walls could not leak *silent talk*
could not reveal words about a life on the run

or following *the plan*. Planks in walls could not
tell about the magic of the northern star.

Floors could not reveal unexpressed farewells
marked in dust by leaving feet. Nor could they talk
of new runaways, or where danger was, or where
winter food was hidden.

Silent talk cautioned, seal your lips. Dance. Show joy
to the master. The walls have ears. Retribution listens.
Don't tell about the blond slave girl escaped north,
now an unmarried doctor with brown eggs in
    her womb.
Family history is sealed.

Plowing

Austin Fray (December 8, 1875–October 24, 1924)

What did your mother tell you about our poppa?
—Aunt Edna

My mother said her poppa
was a wall of a man,
was a brick mason, helped build
the school at Stony Point,
had a lap large enough
for all of his children and more.
Her poppa could predict rain
like the animals could,
was a farmer who loved the smell
and feel of the hard red

Virginia clay,
had learned to make it yield
the best crops and stock.
Mother thought her poppa
must have known God personally
for God had made her poppa fair.
She thinks it was the earth
that killed him young
or maybe the old women still with
African ways and African thoughts.

The women said her poppa
was too good, was too fair
for a mortal man,
said he'd better watch
not be too great, the gods
are jealous of greatness in men.
On a cold, crimson October day
Mother watched him plowing his fields.
He plowed in rhythm like a symphony.
He plowed to music he hummed.

Her poppa was followed by Jeff, his dog,
was followed by the hired stranger
followed step by step in soft earth.
Even in the rain her poppa plowed
and the stranger followed
step by step in soft earth.
In the morning her poppa
did not rise with the rooster's crow,
her mother's screams,
or the old women's cries.

At her poppa's funeral, my mother
vowed to warn all the men
she would ever love to never trust
smiles of gods, or plow too long,
or walk in soft earth, or let a stranger

follow. The old women say, strangers
mark your grave when they follow
your footsteps in soft, plowed ground.
Mother says, maybe, for good men,
all ground is soft.

Blood of Our Mothers

The Ashanti believe our lifeblood
is from our mothers
and our spirit is from our fathers.
I almost spilled my mother's blood
when I had grown tired and my arms
hurt too much from covering my head
from blows of words.
But on the day I picked, I saw
Great-Grandmother Ellen,
in my bathroom mirror and I was Ellen
boiling and washing laundry not my own,
sewing for the house down the road
and sewing clothing and bonnets,
for my family, while they sleep.
I feel blood heavy in my womb
the new baby, Elenor (my grandmother),
to be born bearing an egg for my mother,
Alice,
and I,
not even a thought,
but already
in the blood.

Roots

*The Cherokees also gathered herbs in the hills
and greens by the water and wild grapes in
the mountains . . .*

—Marion L. Starkey, *The Cherokee Nation*

Alone
I could never identify good.
Common weeds were mystery.
I was pulled awake by the crow
of rooster and mother's voice
and dragged myself to fields
attached to her firm hand.
It is better to gather at dawn,
she said. I stood chest-deep
in wet fields, watched the sun
move from her purple blankets
of mountains and call
the unwrapped day.
Mother stooped,
made her apron a basket,
gathered dandelion and pokeweed
which oozed milky liquid.
No buds today, she said.
Buds should not be bothered.
Let them sleep, until later.
There were wild things harvested

chicory, burdock, mallow, clover.
But mostly I remember green
pokeweed, which performed tangos
in her black pot of steaming water.
When pokeweed was cleansed
by the roll of scalding water
ham hocks joined the untamed
dinner dance. Yet, I am fearful
of food gathered wild from fields,
from between poisonous weeds.
Pokeweed sucks poison from Mother
Earth stores it in elongated finger roots
and in the mouth will paralyze
tongue and speech.

Place

My mother says I'll be quiet. Stay
in *my place.* But I guess I never knew
my place. We have just brought her back
from Virginia where red earth
smells like mint tea and the family

cemetery on the hill has mimosa
and wisteria survivors.
In Virginia she flourished, an oak tree
in a forest of fire devoured pines.
We tell her she cannot live

in the south, because Virginia
sunsets burst like blood vessels
over blue hills and air is so sharp
and clear it jars our city lungs.
She laughs. I still have memory.

I remember Grandmother Ellen didn't
know her place. I don't know mine, so
I'm not runoff water running away
to a stagnant pond. Place. There's
place and there's Home.

Grandmother Ellen was put off
The Plantation. She didn't fit
like a person of her color, was all

mouth, talked white, talked about
freedom to the slaves. She stuck out,

a sunflower in a cotton field,
called her husband Mr. Lewis
because the south called him boy.
On our land at Stony Point Grandmother
Ellen and her husband Grand had sons:

Charlie, James, John, and Edgar
and daughters: Elizabeth, Lucy,
Virginia, Lillian, Cornelia,
and my mother, Elenor.
They never fit any mold.

Mother's Tin Box

In the October days, after Mother died, I sorted
boxes and bags musky with age; they bulged
with her saved days. She could not save herself
from her bulging veins and weakened heart.

Concealed among her things, I found an English
toffee tin *Made in England.* Painted on the top
II giardino dell' Amore by *Paul Rubens*
puffy angels cavorting in spaces over

a summer garden party.
Like Pandora I opened Mother's box.
In the tinned protected space, folded
in crumbling, creamy tissue paper a love poem

clipped from the newspaper, antiqued by time,
MAKING HER MEANING CLEAR
When he had made his earnest plea
She gazed far off and thought awhile

I wish that I could say the word—
But others today have erred,
by letting kindness have its way—
Was it a poem she had received or saved

for a man? My father? Not my father?
Also in her gilded box were pictures of people

I had not known, but looked like me.
In one photograph, under a full-leafed maple tree

my mother is young, suspended in the sunny woods
of time. Her long black hair, undone, was loosely
wrapped around her tilted head. Like a sapling
in the wind she leaned toward the smile of a man

offering a look I'd only seen reflected
in my mirror on my wedding day.
Why did I think she only knew my father
or bending over a washtub full of dingy cares

and children's clothes, or standing like a cipher
formed by pain in front of her cookstove
with banked fires? When I search my box
of memories, I'll not see an aged seamed face,

fragile limbs, a long gray braid and dying,
but remember her box, *Il giardino dell' Amore*,
a young girl, hair undone, a poem,
and what was saved in a photograph.

Cooking Rice in a Home
While Dreams Sleep

Rice, each grain an argument. Daddy, you demanded
white rice. Mother cooked it reluctantly, married
it with red beans bearing the name of the organ,
which later betrayed you. *Rice is better for bones,*
you insisted. Mother choose silence as her weapon,
wanted Virginia potatoes with red dirt flaked away
by her thumbs. We grew bones from both foods
cooked and served on plates of impending storms.
During dinners, Daddy, you reminded us the cost
of dreams, purchased by your depression paychecks
earned from work on the WPA. You helped build
highways you would never drive. Your dream
of being a lawyer was hod you carried
on your shoulders. It did not bend them. Hodman,
helper to master builders, you carried in your lunch
bucket invisible words, Dubois, Dunbar, law:
constitutional, mosaic.
You waited for a slip in time for return of dreams.
We children also waited on summer evenings
for Friday payday treats. Daughters awake, learning
lessons of patience. Your sons gave up,
were asleep in bed. We girls slapped mosquitoes,
scratched blood, whispered anticipation.
You staggered home with crumpled paper bags
        of treats.
The words thrown between you and Mother smacked

at our ears. But they didn't stop the joy of our greed
—anticipated goodies.
Daddy, for you, I have made dreams a priority; they are
your rice, tiny grains each lifted from a black pot,
slow-cooked and nourishing.

Fireflies, How You Wear Them

The ticks of an invisible clock.
We sisters afraid of the dark sit
on the bottom step of our clapboard
house under a blue-black sky.
Overhead are, *can almost touch stars.*

Fireflies on a Saturday night with nuggets
of gold fly in lazy patterns above our heads.
We chatter softly in the seashore breeze.
Daddy will be here soon. He said so.
We keep voices too low to carry upstairs.

Two little girls with firefly bracelets,
one little girl, with a double firefly anklet
up past curfew, wait for Daddy and frost-
covered Popsicles: double sticks, lemon,
cherry, grape, Daddy's laugh, Daddy's stories.

Mother calls. Silence. Little girls wait for promises.
Then, *Daddy! Daddy is here. Daddy!*
One little girl, *Thanks, Daddy.*
Daddy, a pungent figure, sways in the breeze;
his smile is blurred in the night. Under the porch

light, he offers a brown paper bag caramel colored,
wet, almost breaking. Popsicles are swirls
of sticky warm liquid. Double sticks float with

useless promises. One little girl, *That's not Popsicles.*
Another little girl, in her mother's voice,

Where have you been? They are all melted.
The little girl with the firefly anklet, almost in tears,
It's okay, Daddy. We can drink them like Kool-Aid.
We did. Daddy on a summer evening teaches
lessons to little girls with firefly jewelry.

Lions Don't Eat Us

Some nights we gathered around Daddy, pulled stories
from him, dessert to fill half empty bellies. Our Daddy
said he was a religious observer. Said he knew God,
    observed
His workings, and kept an eye on Him. In the kitchen
    Mother
slammed cooking pots, made angry dents in the
    wooden carving
table, said, *Blasphemy!*

We moved closer, pretended not to hear. We needed
    softness.
Times were hard like the day-old rolls made softer
    by vegetable
soup and scalding lemon tea. Daddy read and recited
    Bible stories,
one brow raised in a question mark. With the fables
    of Aesop
he dropped sugar cubes on our tongues. He put a
    finger to his lips,
Don't tell. We begged for more and giggled the sugar
    to liquid.

I left home, married, and had children. When my home
became a hot furnace of betrayal Daddy's words
    returned

and rescued me. Jonah in the belly of a whale, children saved
   from the fiery furnace, Daniel in the lion's den, and the slave,
Androcles, in the emperor's arena. In the days of evening stories
and sugar cubes, Daddy said, *My babies, we're special people,*
lions don't eat us. And they didn't.

Brown Paper Bags

(For my niece, Tina)

Tina reminded me that her grandfather
Charles, my father always seem to carry
a brown paper bag, an extension of his hands,
crumpled as though it had traveled.

I remember Mother and Daddy late
at night, downstairs. Their voices
clashed, carried to our pressed ears
at the heater ducts upstairs.

Mother said, Charles, I'm tired
of your friends, men with low-hung
bellies and your trifling wide-ass
women, Skokie and Sallie, your

speakeasy tramps. You bring bathtub
hooch home in your gut, on your breath
and in those brown paper bags.
Don't you go back to Lou-Anna's den

of iniquity, rotgut liquor, and jazz music.
Daddy laughed promised with all his love
not to return, replaced speakeasies with
the corner bar and crumpled brown bags

which hid *Four Roses,* the pint size.
When I was grown Daddy died; his funeral
on the night Martin Luther King was shot
marked the death of two dreamers.

Martin's dreams articulated to the world
my father's unheard in the roar of living.
In the tears of washing up and putting away
in Daddy's room, hidden under his mattress,

which we were never able to plump,
paper bags of words. They popped up,
stretched, talked loudly. Daddy's life scribbled
from fold to seams, years of words pushed,

squeezed, and fell off to hide in crumpled
pockets of paper. They danced his life:
seashells, Martin, Georgia, freedom, jazz.
There were numbers that never "hit,"

and his favorite number 323 for our college fund.
Once a "combination paid off." We celebrated
with submarines, a long Italian loaf sandwich,
made with combinations of cold cuts and cheese.

That day we gathered and stored Daddy's laughter
behind our eyes.

Medicine Bottles and Baseball

(For my children, Angela and Lynn)

Lynn says,
I am seven in the kitchen of the big house
on Preston Street, Philadelphia. I hug
Grand-Mom, bury my face
in her starched Sunday apron perfumed
with rosemary and dill. Her iron pot of lamb
sizzles on the back of the stove.
Grand-Mom says, *Lynn, go on now. Go play.*
The other kids flood in. Twelve cousins
invading on a Sunday afternoon.
My big sister Angela swats at me as I escape
upstairs to Grand-Pop's room.
Smiling my sister prepares to protect her place
favored, firstborn grandchild, untouchable.
Kitchen smells follow me mingle with peppermint
and pipe tobacco as I jump on Grand-Pop's bed.
He laughs; the bed creaks and smacks the wall
like a Jackie Robinson home run.
I know nothing of cancer and how it is stealing
Grand-Pop's life even as his hero
is stealing home. Grand-Pop loves Jackie Robinson
like his pints of Four Roses hidden under his bed.
Joe Black's father is my friend, he says, grinning.
He invited me to a Dodger game.

He throws a wad of paper like a curved ball.
I catch it and fall down laughing. Two of my cousins
come upstairs. We tumble on the floor on top of pages
of *The New York Times* and *Sunday Inquirer.*
We must wait until the game is over to hear stories:
Grand-Pop's *Othello,* Frederick Douglass,
Booker T. Washington, and Martin Luther King.
I fiddle with his medicine bottles trying to read names
foreign and hard on the tongue. He says, *Sound them out.*
They're no good. They don't make sense anyhow.
He gets into his silence. He closes his eyes.
I pry them open like I do my sister's dolls.
He laughs so hard he sheds tears.
Later that next spring, when the pills and Grand-Mom
could not longer keep him here or take the pain
he closed his eyes and I was not there to pry them open.

Prophecy

On my back porch, in shadows of decades-old
maples, in this season when butterscotch leaves
swim down from bones of maple, twist on wind
currents, and lie at peace on the ground,
I sense my father beside me on the swing.
He has returned today in our birth-month
to share the shift of seasons. Daddy says noisy
leaves remind him of the time, when as a child
on his native island, his mother led him
through menacing sounds of a Georgia night
to visit Dr. Raven, the voodoo man.
Grandma went through thickets down a path
between inverted bottles in trees toward chants,
grunts of farm animals, and owls hooting.
She waited her turn while Daddy squirmed
like the restless leaves above his head.
Dr. Raven appeared in smoke in a snow-white suit
wearing a bright red mask over his face.
He prophesized twice a year and was truth
in a world of myths and white-man's laws.
Daddy said, he told him he would leave south
on a circus train with a cover of flying geese,
go north, predicted he would leave water,
be followed by water, and would see fire fall
from December skies dropped
by huge black birds with open bellies.

Foretold he would see hail in summer
and pictures appear in a box without wires,
have twenty sons and daughters, see
a two-headed cow, touch ice mountains that walk,
and be remembered with a murdered man
he'd never met.
Daddy swore the next day when he went
with his dad to a farm to exchange corn and flour
for meat the bloody hands that steadied the scales
of beef and pork were those of the voodoo man.
I have learned shadow is sometimes solid and solid
is shadow and prophecy sometimes truth and truth lies.
Maybe this is what I should have remembered
in the throbbing March night when we memorialized
Daddy in a Philadelphia church and Martin Luther King
died in Tennessee and the two flowed into each other.

Part III

 ## Journeys

It is estimated that 4,809,000 African Americans
left the south from 1900 to 1960 and an estimated
1.5 million left during The Great Migration 1916–1930.

> *When the journey's over*
> *There will be time enough to sleep.*
>
> —A. E. Housman, "Reveille"

The Great Migration

Black families left the south with
burning in their bodies. It was not
a fever but fire paper-fed.
Crops left in fields, sun-scorched
Georgia rice, dried Louisiana
sugar cane, and parched earth below
the Mason-Dixon Line became history.
No leader, but destination led.
Fueled by words of *The Chicago Defender:*
lynching, low wages, southern funerals,
despair erupted into something tangible.
The newspaper smuggled by Pullman
Porters was a fan, was fuel
passed north to south, hand to hand
in barbershops and Black churches.
North to Chicago, Detroit, Philadelphia,
tongues of flames redefined landscapes.
The Industrial Revolution lusted for workers
even the Mississippi spilling over
with families' tears could not stop the push
pull of momentum.
Ahead northern unburned ground,
candescent light, smoke hiss, smolder.
Combustion.

If My Sapling Survives Winter . . .

Georgia, 1916

The white-woman's words hang, caught up
in southern humidity.
You're a good girl, not too much starch
in the collars and cuffs, don't talk back.
Fannie is silent, with lowered head, her face
is ironed smooth with learned ancestral lessons.
She lifts laundry from her cart to the backyard table.
The woman's voice continues, silky smooth,
Listen Fannie; better get your Charlie out of town;
they'll be riding soon.
Fannie bows her covered hair, a fragile yellow rose.
Yes, Ma'am. Thank you, Ma'am. Her voice isn't hers
but something ancient, fractured.
She smiles, closes the garden gate between them.
Her legs are commanded to expected slowness down
the hill; she paces herself like the first few earth-clumps
of an avalanche. At the turn, out of sight, Georgia clay
wet from a summer-morning storm is no match
    for Fannie's
determination. Her feet barely touch the ground.
Her cart bangs her heels. Soon in safety of thick
    pinewoods,
she screams up into menacing clouds. I hate you,
    Creator.

I hate you, God. I hate you as Yahweh. I hate all
    your names.
I hate you, Beliah, you African, for bringing your
    Eastern God
to my husband's Gullah people. You preached hope,
preached power of morning and afternoon prayers to
    the east
but nothing has changed in stealing of children,
    not words
or chains. Trees are my church. They are my
    messengers.
When summer-green leaves whisper and brown
    autumn leaves
tap messages, sooshwan, sooshwan, I believe. I believe
in the bend of their heads and sway of their bodies.
    I listen
as they listen to my screams. Shhhh. Shhhh. I know
if my sapling fig tree survives the winter my son will
    be safe
on his journey up north.

Leaving Home

Georgia, 1916

Such heat of a Georgia day.
At supper I empty the air of silence.
My words are a bone passed around
from sibling to sibling to my parents.
The bone is sucked clean.
Poppa clinches his fists.
Mamma tells of recent warning words
from the white woman over the tracks.
Mamma carried these words home
with the woman's dirty laundry and left
them in the washhouse.
Daily I see slow trains puff their way
north by our house. My best friend
fled last week like that puffed smoke.
In my sixteenth year I must follow
tracks that moan and curve north
to Detroit and in my going must leave
my family innocent.
My big sister pushes back her chair
leaves the table, pulls down the flour sack,
dusts the board white, pounds with two fists
the light bread for tomorrow.

Sleeping Where Elephants Dance

Charles Henry Quarterman Jr., Georgia, 1916

This train clanks steel on steel.
A tight metal ball in my gut dissolves
as I live names of northbound states
my father taught me like walking.
Sixteen years old spring in my bones
and my parents lose their only son
to the open mouth of a northbound circus train.
In a diamond-roped sky the moon hangs low.
Southern locals are deprived of Friday's sport.
In this slatted car I share with elephants
I pull my quilt of *flying geese** tightly
around my trembling, inhale familiar scents
of my pipe-smoking grandmother.
I relive her last hug and feel her pushing
the bundle of quilt, biscuits, and cheese
into my hands. Her jug of lemonade is still cool.
I touch my medicine bag from my mother.
My father's Gullah amulet hangs concealed,
around my neck, under my shirt.
Peels of red and yellow paint drift from walls
of the swaying car, fall on me and feet of elephants

> **flying geese: a quilt pattern utilized by slaves to show*
> *time to run away*

delicate in their dance around my straw bed.
Dawn, day, evening, night. My divisions of time
blur and grade-school geography becomes reality.
Tennessee, trails of pungent tobacco in drying sheds.
In the dark, elephant manure dumped in fields.
Kentucky, barns, paintings in bronze sunset
are home to sleek thoroughbreds. Circus mules
and scarred diving horses awaken with kindred smells.
We shimmy into rain and smoky air of Ohio's
        factories.
Strange metallic voices mutter curses at the rain.
I wipe down the elephants; refill their water tanks,
stand in rain, wash off the last of southern dust.
I wait with amens, a medicine bag, and a little god.
Michigan, our train coughs and shudders
to its final destination, Detroit.
I am led by beats of my thumping heart,
and a congregation of acrobats and clowns.

Traveling North

Family said Daddy lived briefly in the
New England states after he left the south.

My father was feet going north
into cold faces of snow-colored strangers.
Two feet going north into kitchens
of sailors' rooming houses full of tales:
ancient pyramids, ant hills as tall as southern
silos, mean herds of elk north in Nova Scotia,
white bears wild and musky in cities of ice.
He was two feet going north wrapped
in insistent northern sounds that finally
smothered his southern speech.
Two feet going north with slap, slap, slap
of loose soles on Massachusetts, Maine,
and Rhode Island streets.
New England factories belched black smoke
and expelled foul green air from open pipes.
Daddy was in its heaving guts in absent daylight
where metal grated on metal hotter than hottest
Georgia summers left behind.
On a Tuesday when dawn dragged coldness
into the inhospitable day he purchased glue
and new soles for his shoes then started
walking south to Philadelphia and the man
he was to become.

Detroit

(1916)

Your smoky scent is musky
in my nose.
A metal taste is loud in these
cafés and jook joints.
Foreign food and foreign
faces make me long for home.

I want to be your child,
lie on your breast, hear
your heartbeat, feel
damp warm skin beneath
your blouse. I want
comfort from your arms.

My journey has been long.
I am a dark-skin man-child.
My feet still track southern clay.
Kinfolk cried when I left home,
said their arms were not strong
enough to hold me.

Father smiled, urged me to go.
I saw friends leave wagons
standing in streets
and cram northern trains.

I left boll weevils, floods, dying
crops, and cruelty.

I have grown to love you, Detroit.
I don't want to be your child.
I want to be your lover,
to feed you
Georgia grits in exchange
for your grit and glamour.

I love your clanks and bangs,
hammering and wheels.
I love your whistle voice
calling men to you.
I love your acid smell of paint.
I love the smudge of your lips.

Your smoke black hair
doesn't rest on your shoulders
but rises up in plumes.
Your slate gray eyes
pierce the black night.
In the morning you arise
fluids flowing and body oiled

sleek and ready to stretch
farther and faster than

the fastest racehorse.
You have a hunger for men
with strong bodies, hands,
legs, and muscles.

I can be that, fresh unending
work, hands and muscles,
a body primed for labor.
Only let me rest in evenings
on your breast and test the steel
of your thighs.

June 1917 Letter from Philadelphia,
This City Sings

Mother Bethel A.M.E. Church, Philadelphia,
said in a leaflet sent south circa 1917, Let this be
your home.

Dear Poppa,

Finally Philadelphia. I have moved my life
here with diploma, your wool cap and coat.
In threads of light we ran from the dark smelly train.
Southern laughter overflowed into domed
      Broad Street
Train station. Sam and I were almost struck dumb
by hulking giant stone gray buildings, many-eyed
with windows. What a strange, wondrous place this is.
Cousin Jeff has rented me a room and sends greetings.
I work in a slaughterhouse for wages.
I don't need anything. *Mother Bethel Church*
welcomed Sam and me with open arms.
I still miss our church and singing in the choir.
Philadelphia sings in trolley altos, soprano car-
squeaks, tenor bells and clamor.
This city is a checkerboard of languages
a patchwork of communities fashioned by hands
of migrants and immigrants.
I smell cabbage, chicken coops, and cinnamon bread.
Houses are attached side by side like rowed beads.

I fear if Philadelphia shakes its shoulders
cobblestones and houses will roll down the street,
crush trolleys on their tracks, or continue tumbling
into the mouth of the Delaware River.
During the week I long to turn down city sounds
by the pull of a switch.
Sunday mornings God must smile on this city
of churches and church voices soft on the air.
Sabbath evenings on the steps of our house
on Kenilworth Street, Jeff, Sam, and I count our wages
and plan our lives like planting summer crops
            for harvest.
We know our journey was not everything. In shops on
Market Street, the waterfront, rich people's houses and
slaughterhouses, we are the question marks on the brow
of Philadelphia, unknown southern coloreds changing
the face of the city.

                                        Your loving son, Charlie

February 1918 Letter from Philadelphia, Caesar Lee

Dear Poppa,

There is a crepe hanging on our door.
Caesar Lee is dead. Did I tell you about Caesar Lee?
I met him in church. He sang like heaven's angels
must sound. He came to live in our rooming house.
Licorice skin and tall from Mississippi.
He had his own picture of this world painted in colors
on the inside of his eyes: salmon-tinted western skies,
blue waters, crystal snowflakes, each handmade by God.
Up early to hear birds before city sounds, he liked
midnight stars almost as much as Miss Lucy's
     café lights.
Women loved him like chocolate ice cream.
Before Philadelphia, on a ripe spring day he waited
for a westbound train to Iowa where his uncle was.
Desperate white farmers snatched him from the station,
bound him like a slave. Made him harvest dying crops
day and night. Beaten and weak, almost dead,
     he escaped
swam a muddy Mississippi, like a catfish.
Sailors pulled him from the river, nursed him, brought
him to Philadelphia, left him on the banks of the
     Delaware.
He was seduced by the city; her strident voice,
     her people.

Caesar's body was fractured. Still every day like sun
rising, he said, *Dreams, I got dreams. I'm growing
myself new here in Philadelphia. Yes. Yes. Yes!*
I wanted him to have dreams, wanted him to hold on.
But he was like an acorn on an oak; he had to fall.
Spring courted him. Summer loved him. Fall deceived.
Winter killed. Not just pneumonia, but southern evil
northern cold, chilled bones, and weakened body.
At the cemetery, snowflakes decorated his pine box.
We sang *His Eye Is on the Sparrow* and *Nobody
Knows the Trouble I've Seen*. Ice-crusted trees cracked.
Women moaned wind sounds.
Poppa, I got a pay raise today. What do you need?
Did you get the boots I sent?
This rooming house is too quiet.
I didn't know, something like *dreams,* something
like that. Something you can't see or hear or feel
can be so noisy and leave such quiet.

Your loving son, Charlie

September 1923 Letter from Philadelphia, About Salt and Sugar

Dear Poppa,

How are you and Mamma? I miss you so much.
I miss faces, Mamma, I miss sweet potato pie.
I start this letter in my head as on clean paper
while walking my usual five miles to work.
This September day is perfect, in need of nothing.
At the site white men in overalls spill
like salt from noisy trolleys. Soon as he sees me
Boss man hollers, *Hey, Boy, you there, hurry*
get me some coffee.
I like plenty of sugar, can you remember that?
Yes, Boss, I say and nod.
Tomorrow I leave this job for college. My secret
hidden for now, like a baby in a womb.
I pour his cup, blessings of coffee smells invade
my nose and I am reminded of you, Poppa,
each morning a cup, each morning a prayer
for living of the day and protection of family.
Boss man yells, *Sugar, no cream, sugar.*
My hand has its own life, pauses, finds a blue tin
of white crystals, lifts three spoons, pours them
into brown liquid to be dissolved and coffee
is forever changed, but not that the eye can see.
Boss man jerks his cup from my hand,
turns his back, slurps loudly, then yells, his mouth

a sewer of words, *Damn you, damn, you're all dumb,*
can't read, can't understand nutting, like animals.
I got to do everything myself. This here is salty!
He hurls coffee from his cup; steaming, it spills itself
into the earth, sinks, wets parched trampled ground.
Black earth, at least at this spot, is changed, is renewed.
I pour my coffee into my own mug, wrapped in
     its aroma
I lift sweetness from the tin, sugar my coffee three
     spoons
the way you taught me, Poppa, syrupy and energizing
for a need-nothing day like this.

                    Your loving son, Charlie

The Journey Home

I'm certain we are too far north.
Our driver says he knows
where he is going.
But we are lost, I know textures
of lost, arms stretched out,
nothing solid to touch,
landmarks absent, blanks

in a dream of cotton, no sound,
wheels turned in darkness,
dead-end streets,
the wrong direction
on the back roads of New Jersey.
Our headlights tear open spaces
in the fog of small-town ghosts.

Old ghosts are disturbed
as in Ghana's slave castles.
I thought I left them there.
Finally the driver stops, asks
directions, finds the road,
Garden State Parkway south.
I never knew I liked this parkway,
cars, noise, congestion,

like congestion from the cold I caught
at Hotel President, Yamoussoukro

in Côte d'Ivoire amid splendor, damp
with green-gray mildew of dungeons.
The passage home takes
nine hours snail-like progress
threaded through summer traffic.

On the plane from Africa, I slept
the seven and one half hours
from Dakar, Senegal.
In this time, inched away, being lost,
I could have returned to Africa
like a thrown boomerang
to bounce off red soil.

I didn't know I loved red soil,
red clay soil of my grandparents' farm
when northeast Washington, D.C.
had room for farms.
I learned to love rusty Virginia soil
where my mother returned
to the southern cocoon of her birth

and was transformed
like larva to a butterfly.
We travel south toward salt marshes.
I didn't know how much I loved
salt marshes, salt on tongue, on skin.

At Pink Lake in Senegal, where salt
comes up from the face of the lake

like reverse snow, among salt piles
numbered and marked by laborers,
I tasted salt on my lips, like salt
of soft pretzels from vendors
on streets of Philadelphia.
The fall leafy smells
of New Jersey fires

and scents of African wood smoke
will haunt me with remembrance
of our meals cooked over charcoal.
The cremation of trees is completed,
the circle of life is continuous,
in the death of Africa's
wood scraps.

I burn wood in my fireplace
for sensual pleasure. I do not kneel
before fire to cook or pray. I honor water.
So I walked into the Atlantic Ocean
by the Slave House of Gorée;
my chained body unchained,
filled and empty, returned home.

Part IV

 Ancestors' Stories, Myths, and Rituals

*When the last Red Man shall have perished, and the
memory of my tribe shall have become a myth among the
white man, these shores will swarm with the invisible dead
of my tribe . . . At night when the streets of your cities and
villages are silent and you think them deserted, they will
throng with the returning hosts that once filled them . . .*

—Chief Seattle

Language of Love

African Journal, Wednesday,
August 7, 1996

On the road to Togo,
land of the mysterious
we pass roadblocks,
forced pauses
on our journey.
During one stop,
women, fruit piled
on heads
in colored patterns,
surround our bus.
We are enclosed
in fragrance, soft
unfamiliar, familiar
voices and color.
One woman stands out,
tall, ebony, shades darker
than Great-Grandmother,
but is Great-Grandmother.
Her eyes lock mine.
Eloquent hands gesture.
She touches black
encyclopedic eyes,

her heart, her mouth,
points to me, signs
in universal language.
I love you.
Welcome home!

Smoking Leaf

Grand—(James Lewis) had many skills. He was a weaver and he also grew tobacco, made it into plugs and twists which he sold.

—Mother

In a valley in Virginia
Great-Grandfather, red
with southern dirt
wooed earth for crops.
His first cabin squatted
by fragrant fields
of tobacco leaves.
His Cherokee eyes
squinted to test sun strength
as he braided and bound
his long black hair.
Sharp bird voices jeweled
air with melodies.
Katydids sang. Often
Great-Grandfather stood
in puffs of dawn
and thanked gods
for the smoking leaf.
As he moved
among his tobacco plants
selecting leaves

his picking was
as gentle as his hand
upon grandchildren's heads.
In peaceful night,
copper-coated by moon,
radiant, in amber glow
of his smoking, he wove
tales of pipes passed
in darkened rooms.
History was drawn
upon walls and floor:
how his father
was given the smoking leaf.
He said, once men were gods
and gods, men, who blew
fire into earth's belly,
patted mountains
into peaks, scraped-out
valleys with fingernails,
squeezed glacier shapes
through their toes,
and placed a glowing
pipe in the sky as moon
to guide hunters
safely home.
When his braids

were white and he wore
out like once fertile earth,
he was buried
beside his tobacco fields
at his home place
in Stony Point.
Fires were banked,
ashes scattered, became
earth, became history
in that place where sweet
moist smoke once rose
from drying sheds.

Thunderbird

(A Native American legend from my mother)

From the land of things
which do not sleep
from the crown
of green mountain hair
of the Thunder god
comes Thunderbird.
Her shadow
is the storm cloud.
Wind screams her flight.
Bullroarer in her throat
she whizzes sound
in waves
spews it from her beak.
Her talons sprout
lightning, which
leaps from her heart.
Her lightning
illuminates,
splits and strikes.
On her back a bag of lakes
spill, splash waterfalls.
Her wings flap thunder.
Sound compressed
to thunder roars down

on roads of rocks and light.
Her feathers are soft
bits of iridescence;
and are her children,
which cling, travel
on her body, her thighs,
and outspread wings
to learn her ways.
Thunderbird hovers
like a last breath,
dips down, trails light,
leaves acid thunder smells
leaves burnt pain of wounding.
> *We are her multi-colored children.*
> *My mother is the Red granddaughter.*
> *I am the mixed Black great-granddaughter*
> *Thunderbird's fledgling, learning wings.*

I Will Not Be Remembered

Removal began, 1838 (Trail of Tears)

I am Tsali's wife.
No one will remember my name.
My life is hummingbirds' wings
which beat against the face of the Infinite.
I am empty of children and beauty.
I am wife to the man who became warrior
in his old age, when he shielded me
from a soldier's bayonet. The soldier died.
Hunted animals, driven by the Georgia militia,
we fled and now hide in these Carolina hills.

In youth we did drink the earth
and laced ourselves soul to soul.
We were lovers who married this land.
The shape of our bodies fit perfectly
before they curved their own way in age.
My skin was fair, my legs a marvel.
I no longer love these slow legs.
These legs that once outran men,
caught rabbits on the run, stumbled,
failed when I needed them.

Come, old man, lie with me
on our petaocawin. Entwine your
spirit with mine. We will anchor

each other for a new journey.
I am ill. I am in this time of the long night.
Tonight I will die as my sisters and brothers
on the trails below these caves.
Here in these hills we are coward safe,
but not cowards. This is too much!
Tomorrow on your journey down

to the militia's bullet, remember, you give
your body as the buffalo gives his life.
Long after tomorrow, the meat of your being
will be food for our people's minds.
Your story will be horns and skin, proud
headdress for a warrior.
My husband, old man, I'll wait for you
where life begins and ends. Good night, love.
Tomorrow crouches on her haunches, waiting.

The Legend of Tsali

*During the removal of Cherokee from their
homelands, Tsali defended his wife; a soldier
was shot accidentally.*

I am an old man, my bones creak
like dry sticks rubbed together.
My wife has gone to the spirit world.
From my hiding place here in the hills
I witness the white man make sores
on our land. How can heaped-up scars
heal deep gouging of Mother's golden veins?
I will give my life for my sons, willingly,
like the white missionary's Abraham
offered up his son for blessings.
Tell this to my brothers who have gone
to the land of the west, where the Dark
Death man lives, in the death house.
I go to what the white man calls death.
I will not die; wind never dies.
Breath becomes air and air breath.
My seeds will not die; they will reseed
our lands with children who carry my face.
I pass to another world, for I am tired.
My spirit is ready for the journey.
Listen for me at night in rustled leaves.
I'll be shadow. I'll be sound.

Listen for me at night in calls of owls.
Look for me in sunshine where
my grandchildren play on Cherokee
spirit-hallowed grounds.
Look for me in light.

Gorée, Island of Infamy

(West Africa, August 5, 1996)

Something terrible happened here.
Bones of my bones, teeth
of my teeth line this Atlantic floor.
Ripped apart, like clams, families
captured, chained in transport
jumped into this sea to declare:
better flesh becomes shark food
than pass through
The Door-of-No-Return
better immediate death than distant
demise in white-winged sea monsters.
Today, I bathe in Africa's Atlantic
where something terrible happened.
Salt-soaked spirits arise, follow
slave ships, human cargo stuffed
in their bulged gut, spoon-fitted, space.
The fetid air is whipped by despair
and restless spirits whisper names
of ancestors, beg continuance
of infant names given up to waters,
given back to sea gods, *Ife, Layla, Mosi.*
I revere your names, honor you,
call out my name to you, as gull

calls out to gull.
Mother of Great-Grandmother's bones,
father of Great-Grandfather's bones
you put oceans in me and I'm drawn
to watery graves where ancestors lie.

Betrayal of Breasts

*A girl would be considered a maiden if her
breast held up firm. An ancient African custom
the slave traders . . . borrowed . . . to sell . . .
slave girls.*

—Boubacar Joseph Ndiaye, Principal Curator
of the Slave House, Gorée Island, Senegal

Better I should cut off my breast
than follow my sisters to Gorée.
Better I should anger my gods
than be snared by my body.
Should I be betrayed by breasts
which have not felt babies'
or lover's lips?
Mother God, pull down my breasts.
Suck from them the life, which makes
them point up to entice captor's eyes.
Let them fall thin, empty, sucked,
dried bosoms of my grandmothers.

Baobab Tree

In musky August air, in a courtyard,
by the slave house on Gorée Island,
there is a tree larger than four of me.
I press my body against its rough skin,
try to feel and hear its memories
of that terrible time of tearing away.
Inside its protected heart, ancient rings
silently formed. In dungeons,
clanking iron rings held separate the
chained children, mothers, and fathers.
Captured, they remembered their tree god,
wailed prayers for deliverance,
called on a god of limbs, leaves, and roots.
This tree's sticky glue-grip could not hold
Ewe or Yoruba from *the trip without return.*
This thirsty tree could not drink enough sea
to keep them safe. Like serpents, neck
and wrist rings grew tighter on bruised flesh,
bound them closer than Baobab glue.
Now in chatter of leaves, I whisper,
Baobab, tree of life, how could you free them
when our great God never stopped the sin?

Arms of Jesus

African slave castles,
Gorée, Cape Coast
and Elmina
stone-faced sisters
still on the full breast
of our Motherland.
I hear your history.
Blasted by ocean,
soaked by tears
not tears of Christ
but ancestors' tears.
Ancestors abducted,
bartered for iron,
traded for brewed spirits,
African spirits. Black
bodies are sorted, weighed.
Children, men, women
are all stored cargo, packed
in the dungeon's entrails
under floors
of dancers' feet.
Not the light of Christ.
Not the body of Christ.
Feeble light threaded
through holes in walls.
Light squeezed into dark.

Light not the aura of Mary.
They pass through *The-Door
of-No-Return*
into holds of slave ships
into the body
of slave ships
into *Jesus**
under the *Crown**
of *Jesus*
into the *Green Dragon.**
into hell.

* *Jesus, Crown, Green Dragon: names of slave ships*

Skeletons

We walked among the people through a fishing
village on our way to Elmina slave castle.
An old woman smiled at me, nodded her head.
My Africa Journal, August 1996

Hey, look over here, African
American woman, on your way
to tour Elmina Slave Castle.
You walk toward the bridge
to cross over from us like
the tide going out.
This is an ancient village.
We are ancient people, ancient
with memories of our children,
children rooted up like wheat,
sorted, stored for shipment.
Hey, look over here, African
American woman. I am your
past left here in this village
by the side of this Atlantic sea.
Death stench of grouper
and snapper find your nose;
their skeletons lay in my streets.
Does something forgotten stir you?
Soupy red clay sucks, pulls
your feet, sticks like Baobab

glue you cannot leave behind.
I am an eye of your ancestors.
Hey, look over here, African
American woman, I see you
returning to my shores.
I am the old woman who is skin
of your ancestors. I am your relation,
your anchor, left here on the Gold Coast
of your Motherland.
Your African bones are exposed
like fish skeletons.
I know you.

Translations

Hidden by the lush pregnant
bulge of Cape Verde
is Île de Gorée
where slave houses
called castles, cling like sores
on the body of Mother Africa.
Gorée, once called "Goede Reede,"
translated Safe Haven,
is child of barter and trade.
Purchased with Dutch iron
bars, it is forged with shame.
Slave houses called castles
were many on Île de Gorée.
In Elmina Castle, concealed
by a turn in a wall, I see
stained, rust-colored neck irons
and in bowels of Cape Coast Castle
sea breezes beg entry
at tiny barred windows.
From holy crumbling walls
my fingers scratch green mold
fixed like scabs.
In the harbor a gull screams
a woman's scream.
The sound grates a language
translated by marks
on the chain-scarred floors.

Braiding

Mothers, daughters share
time; make braids the living
chains, genetic memories.
Daughters, granddaughters
are held between firm Black
thighs. Strands hold together.
Gather up, brush, comb, wrap,
plait, like Mamma, like Nanna.
Our braids reach back in time,
twist like thick chains to lost
years, to African roots, almost
forgotten patterns. Our fingers
remember, continue coils
and delicate patterned strands
of history.

Generations

(For Herbert Jr. who visited Stony Point home place with Aunt Edna in 1998.)

—Aunt Edna's story

My great-nephew Herbert, with a quick
flick of wrist turns from Monticello
onto the narrow road to Stony Point.
Ash-colored skies follow us. In my mind
I push the name around with difficulty
like a rock. The store at the foot of the hill
no longer squats beside the oak tree where
as a boy my brother Ralph, almost
a hundred years ago, carved his name
in rebellion. Later, at the door of that store
we inhaled integrated scents, peppermint
sour balls and smoky Virginia ham.
At the home place, not far away
I try to see through Herbert's eyes
this place we loved, farmed,
harvested crops of beans, collards,
and childhood memories. In later
years my sister, his grandmother Alice
returned here to live the circle of her life.
Since her death, the land has become
yellow with fennel and goldenrod.
Small oak and pine have erupted

from the hard red clay. There remains
a pink rambling rose planted by my
grandmother Ellen.
The roof of my sister's mobile home
is collapsed. From the living room a slender
silver-leaf poplar grows. Only the foundation,
built from red rock brought from these
Virginia mountains, is unbroken.
This is a newborn, unfamiliar south.
The other south I knew is in history
books peopled with oaks, roped laden.
A root catches my foot and reminds me
of the way of roots.
Even as they are pulled, some fragments
will start to grow unseen.
My nephew surveys our land with his eyes.

The Price of Land

*I would ask that my family carry on for me, this
promise I made to Grand (James Lewis) not to
sell the land to anyone outside of the family.*
—from My Mother's journal

*To us the ashes of our ancestors are sacred and
their resting place is hollowed ground.*
—Chief Seattle upon surrendering his land
to Governor Isaac Stevens in 1855

April, Azalea Festival in Virginia,
and we are drenched with pinks,
reds and whites of Charlottesville.
Giddy with spring, we read
street signs on private roads,
trail laughter at bold, telling names,
Pinch Em Slyly, Happy Creek,
Shouters Lane, Lovers Lane.
Left turn, the winding road goes
pass ruins of the country store,
a dinosaur, where once colored adults
called the owner's children
mister and mistress.
Hurried breaths away, we slow down,
stop. Now years after Mother's death
at her Stony Point home place,

I stand on land edged with white pine
and barriers of brush and fence.
Successive times two trucks pass
southern slow, without greeting,
go around the road's bend,
disappear like country dust.
In silence broken by bird calls,
sounds of brakes intrude.
Soon steps. Brush crackles, parts.
A pale farmer's face, a grimy hand
extended.
Once there was a yellow house here
then a mobile home.
His finger points his statement.
A bee drunk with wild plum nectar
circles me. I sense danger.
I answer, *The yellow was my grandfather*
Fray's house.
I turn toward the mobile's remains
a skeleton of a bird, anchored by wires.
Our mother returned here,
lived in the mobile; she is dead.
He fills the silence.
See the rocks on the driveway.
I helped your mother build that driveway.
I fenced this in. I look out for you.

He stands back; his eyes weigh us, red dirt
rims his expectant smile.
I would like to bring in hay for my cattle
use your land for feeding. I'll take care of it.
A tree branch falls, cracks like bones.
Behind us a graveyard, our family's,
under water, under cow dung.

Ancestors

Arms too full of toys
for carrying stories
about ancestors
we complained
when mother stopped us.
She said there was room
and proceeded
to pile stories, nose-high,
left peepholes for us
to look out find our way
through piles of fabric,
>   colored
>
>   woven
>
>   worn
>
>   worn-out
>
>   hung
>
>   burned
>
>   buried
>
>   remembered.
>
>   Ancestors.

Author's Notes

We did not have television. We had one radio.
For hours my mother told us stories of her great-
grandparents, grandparents, and parents. I don't know
what I would have retained if mother hadn't left a
written record of family history. The Lewis and Fray
poems are based on her notes, stories, Family Scrolls
(records of births, deaths, and marriages, dating back
to the 1800s), information from the Virginia Historical
Society, the archives in Richmond, and family stories
supplied by Mother's sister, Aunt Edna.

I have recently started to research my father's family
history. Daddy left Georgia on a circus train during
the great migration, when he was sixteen. He traveled
north from the low country. I am certain if we could
ask my father he would say his journey was his own
and not about history. My father's poems about the
Quartermans are based on family stories, conjecture,
and ongoing research.

Orenda*

From scooped earth
on the sixth day
in the image of God
we became.
From deep black clay,
from divine thought
we came.
From heat of sun,
cold wind, damp breath,
before they were named,
we came.
We flow together
mighty, old, like the Nile,
deep like the Mississippi.
Spirit embraces spirit
one soul, one race,
one remembrance.

*(O-ren'-da—Iroquois word for the spirit that flows
through and connects all beings and elements of the world)*

My Family:

Great-Grandmother Rhoda Randolph, from the Songhai people of Mali, Africa, child of slaves, married Albert Fray, mulatto, by "jumping over the broom," Easter in Virginia. They had five children: John, Rosa, Mary, Alice, and Austin Fray, my grandfather.

Great-Grandmother Ellen Taylor, mixed Cherokee, married James Lewis, Cherokee, circa 1864 in Virginia. They had ten children: John Henry, Virginia, Edgar, Elizabeth, Lucy, Lillian, Cornelia, James Jr., Charles, and Elenor, my grandmother. Elenor Lewis married Austin Fray in Virginia June 8, 1898. They had six children: Lillian, Viola, Ralph, Ada, Edna, and Alice, my mother.

My mother Alice married Charles Jr., my father, son of Charles Henry Sr. and Fannie Mitchell. Fannie was daughter of Paul Mitchell and Amanda Harper. Amanda Harper was Cherokee, who lost kinfolk on the Trail of Tears. Charles Sr. was the son of Narcissus Davis and Pauldo Quarterman. Pauldo Quarterman was the son of Celia Wilson and Simon Quarterman. Celia was the daughter of Tom Wilson and Lyra. They were of the Gullah culture from Georgia and South Carolina by way of Bini, Nigeria.

Alice Fray and Charles Henry Quarterman, my parents, had ten children, Christine, Alphonso, Constance, Geraldine, Kathleen, Herbert, Joseph, Paul, Shirley, and Edward.

As with Aesop's Roman slave, Androcles, who prior to his trial with the lion in the emperor's arena, befriended the lion, we African American families make situations and adversity work for us and survive. LIONS DON'T EAT US.

Constance Quarterman Bridges is the 2005 winner of the Cave Canem Poetry Prize for *Lions Don't Eat Us*. Her work has been published in many journals and magazines, and she has won two fellowships from the New Jersey State Council on the Arts. She currently lives and writes in New Jersey after retiring from the U. S. Treasury Department.

This book was designed by Ann Sudmeier. It is set in
Adobe Caslon Pro type by Prism Publishing Center,
and manufactured by Bang Printing on acid-free paper